Mug Cakes

MADE IN MINUTES IN THE MICROWAVE!

Joanna Farrow

spruce

An Hachette UK Company
www.hachette.co.uk

First published in Great Britain in 2015 by Spruce
a division of Octopus Publishing Group Ltd
Endeavour House, 189 Shaftesbury Avenue,
London WC2H 8JY
www.octopusbooks.co.uk
www.octopusbooksusa.com

Distributed in the US by Hachette Book Group
1290 Avenue of the Americas, 4th and 5th Floors,
New York, NY 10020

Distributed in Canada by Canadian Manda Group
664 Annette St., Toronto, Ontario, Canada M6S 2C8

ISBN: 978-1-84601-491-8

A CIP catalogue record for this book is available from the British
Library.

Printed and bound in China.

10 9 8 7 6 5 4 3 2 1

Both metric and imperial measurements have been given in all recipes.
Use one set of measurements only, and not a mixture of both.

Standard level spoon measurements are used in all recipes
1 tablespoon = 15 ml spoon
1 teaspoon = 5 ml spoon

All microwave information is based on a 650 watt oven. Follow
manufacturer's instructions for an oven with a different wattage.

Eggs should be medium unless otherwise stated. This book contains
dishes made with lightly cooked eggs. It is prudent for more vulnerable
people such as pregnant and nursing mothers, invalids, the elderly,
babies and young children to avoid uncooked or lightly cooked dishes
made with eggs.

This book includes dishes made with nuts and nut derivatives. It
is advisable for people with known allergic reactions to nuts and
nut derivatives or those who may be potentially vulnerable to these
allergies, such as pregnant and nursing mothers, invalids, the elderly,
babies and children, to avoid dishes made with these. It is prudent
to check the labels of all pre-prepared ingredients for the possible
inclusion of nut derivatives.

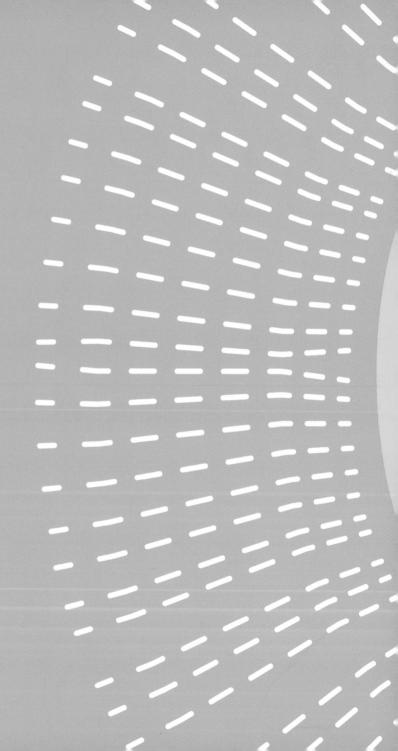

Contents

Introduction

When you crave something sweet but you've no time to bake, treat yourself to a mug cake, the latest craze in quick cooking. Mixed, baked, and eaten from the same mug, they're ready to eat in a matter of minutes. The ingredients are minimal, there are no special pans required, and no wasteful leftovers that tempt you to eat more than you need.

Mug cakes will be appreciated by people of all ages, but they have particular appeal to students and teenagers who can whip up a quick treat that will sustain them for hours. Kids love them as well and it's a great way to get children involved in cooking without the hazards of hot ovens and pans to impede their fun.

Once you've made a few of the recipes in this book, why not try creating your own flavor combinations? Mug cakes don't require very many ingredients, so there's little waste if you don't get it right first time.

CHOOSING A MUG

Before you begin you need to check that the mug you choose is suitable to be used in the microwave. A mug that gets intensely hot before the heat has got to the cake mixture will not cook the cake and may damage the mug. To check that the mug is suitable, fill it with cold water and microwave on full power for 30 seconds. If the mug remains cool but the water has started to heat up, it's probably suitable and you can heat it for a little longer to check that the water gets really hot. If the mug has heated up but the water is still cold or blood heat, the mug won't give good results. Be aware that mugs with metallic edging or decoration usually can't be microwaved.

The recipes in this book use two different mug sizes: 7 fl oz (200 ml) and 12 fl oz (350 ml). The smaller size is good for kids' cakes and richer mixtures. You can use the larger mug for any cake but don't be tempted to use the smaller one in place of the larger one as the mixture is likely to spill over the top and down the side of the mug.

The shape of the mug doesn't really matter, but a sponge cake that will be turned out and sandwiched with filling, such as a Mini Victoria Sponge Cake (see page 10), looks best if the base of the mug is flat, while a pudding-style cake, such as Sticky Syrup Pudding (see page 52), will look better if the base of the mug is rounded, so that the cake has a domed top when turned out.

COOKING TIMES

Microwave cooking times will vary slightly depending on the wattage of the microwave. This can be anything between 600 and 1200 watts. The recipes in this book are designed for a microwave of average wattage, so if your microwave is less powerful then you might need to extend the cooking time fractionally; if higher then slightly reduce the cooking time. Some microwaves don't have an accurate minute timer so you may find it easier to use the stopwatch on your cell phone or a kitchen timer.

Baking Tips

Butter must be really soft so that it's easy to mix with the other ingredients. If you forget to take it out of the refrigerator in time, microwave the measured amount in the mug at medium power in short bursts until the butter is very soft, then add the other ingredients.

•

There's no need to grease the mug or line it with parchment paper. If you're turning the cake out to serve, loosen the edges of the cake with a sharp knife, then place the serving plate face down on top of the mug, invert the mug and plate, and tap the base of the mug to release the cake.

•

Spelt flour can be used instead of regular flour. If the recipe specifies self-rising flour, add a generous pinch of baking powder per tablespoon of spelt flour.

•

The only essential piece of equipment you need is a set of measuring spoons. A very small wire whisk is useful for mixing, though this can also be done with a teaspoon, slim wooden spoon or fork. A toothpick is useful for testing whether a sponge is baked at the end of the cooking time.

Follow the recipe and add the ingredients to the mug in the correct order. Often it's best to add the liquids first so that the dry ingredients don't settle in the edges of the mug, which makes them harder to blend.

●

Unlike traditional baking, there's no lengthy beating or whisking. It's simply a case of blending the ingredients until smooth and lump free. When using a whole egg, as most of the recipes do, make sure it's thoroughly blended into the other ingredients so there are no strands of egg white in the finished cake.

●

Because of their short cooking time, it's very easy to overcook mug cakes, which can make them dry and tough. Follow the suggested cooking times until you become familiar with your own microwave.

●

Ideally, mug cakes are best left for a few minutes after cooking before you eat them. Like all cooked recipes, mug cakes have more flavor when they've cooled a little. Some very sweet ingredients, such as chocolate, fudge, marshmallows, and preserves, are extremely hot when they come out of the microwave so don't bite into cakes straightaway.

●

Although mug cakes are designed as a treat just for one, you can make a few in quick succession for family or friends. Simply line up your mugs and measuring spoons with the ingredients and off you go.

Pistachio and Raspberry Sponge

SERVES 1 • **PREPARATION TIME** 3 MINUTES • **COOKING TIME** 2 MINUTES

Roughly chop the pistachio nuts.

Put the butter, sugar, flour, egg, and chopped nuts in a 12 fl oz (350 ml) microwave-safe mug and beat together until well mixed. Stir in the raspberries.

Microwave on full power for 2 minutes or until the surface feels just firm to touch and a toothpick inserted into the center comes out clean.

2 tablespoons pistachio nuts

3 tablespoons (40 g) unsalted butter, very soft

3 tablespoons superfine sugar

4 tablespoons self-rising flour

1 egg

10 raspberries

Mini Victoria Sponge Cake

SERVES 1 • **PREPARATION TIME** 3 MINUTES • **COOKING TIME** 1½ MINUTES

Beat together the butter and sugar in a 12 fl oz (350 ml) microwave-safe mug. Add the egg yolk, flour, and vanilla extract and beat together until smooth.

Microwave on full power for 1½ minutes or until the surface feels just firm to touch and a toothpick inserted into the center comes out clean.

Loosen the edges of the cake with a sharp knife and turn out onto a plate. Cut the cake in half horizontally, sandwich the layers together with the preserve, and sprinkle generously with sugar.

3 tablespoons (40 g) slightly salted butter, very soft

2 tablespoons superfine sugar, plus extra for sprinkling

1 egg yolk

4 tablespoons self-rising flour

¼ teaspoon vanilla extract

1 tablespoon strawberry preserve

Fig Frangipane Cake with Orange Drizzle

SERVES 1 • **PREPARATION TIME** 5 MINUTES • **COOKING TIME** 2 MINUTES

Put the butter, sugar, ground almonds, almond extract, egg yolk, orange zest, and flour in a 7 fl oz (200 ml) microwave-safe mug and beat together until well mixed.

Cut the fig in half. Roughly chop one half of the fig. Slice the other half of the fig into two pieces and set aside. Stir the chopped fig into the mixture.

Microwave on full power for 1 minute, then place the remaining pieces of fig on top of the sponge and microwave on full power for 1 minute more or until just firm to touch. Drizzle the orange juice and honey over the cake. Serve with cream, if liked.

2 tablespoons (25 g) unsalted butter, very soft

2 tablespoons superfine sugar

¼ cup (25 g) ground almonds

¼ teaspoon almond extract

1 egg yolk

Finely grated zest of ¼ orange

1 tablespoon self-rising flour

1 fresh fig

2 teaspoons orange juice

1 teaspoon honey

Light cream, to serve (optional)

Blueberry, Oat, and Honey Crumble

SERVES 1 • **PREPARATION TIME** 2 MINUTES • **COOKING TIME** 2½ MINUTES

Put the butter in a 7 fl oz (200 ml) microwave-safe mug and microwave on full power for 30 seconds or until melted.

Stir in the oats, sugar, honey, and cinnamon and microwave on full power for 1 minute. Mix well, then stir in the blueberries and microwave for 1 minute more until the blueberry juices start to run. Serve with yogurt.

1 tablespoon unsalted butter

½ cup (50 g) rolled oats

1 tablespoon light brown sugar

2 teaspoons honey

Generous pinch of ground cinnamon

⅓ cup (50 g) blueberries

Greek yogurt, to serve

Poppy Seed and Lemon Cake

SERVES 1 • **PREPARATION TIME** 2 MINUTES • **COOKING TIME** 2 MINUTES

Beat the egg in a 12 fl oz (350 ml) microwave-safe mug. Beat in the oil, lemon curd, sugar, poppy seeds, and lemon zest until thoroughly mixed, then stir in the flour.

Microwave on full power for 2 minutes or until a toothpick inserted into the center comes out clean. Serve topped with extra lemon curd and dusted with a little sifted confectioners' sugar.

1 egg

1 tablespoon vegetable or canola oil

4 tablespoons lemon curd, plus extra to serve

1 tablespoon superfine sugar

1 teaspoon poppy seeds

Finely grated zest of ¼ lemon

4 tablespoons self-rising flour

Sifted confectioners' sugar, for dusting

Rich Chocolate Honeycomb Cake

SERVES 1 • **PREPARATION TIME** 3 MINUTES • **COOKING TIME** 2¾–3 MINUTES

Break the chocolate into a 12 fl oz (350 ml) microwave-safe mug and microwave on medium power for 1–1¼ minutes until melted. Add the butter and stir to make a smooth sauce.

Add the flour, sugar, cocoa powder, and egg and beat until smooth. Microwave on full power for 45 seconds.

Using a rolling pin, lightly crush the honeycomb candies in the bag. Scatter three-quarters of the crushed honeycomb over the sponge and lightly stir in. Microwave for 1 minute more or until just firm to touch. Serve sprinkled with the remaining crushed honeycomb.

1¾ oz (50 g) bittersweet or milk chocolate

2 tablespoons (25 g) unsalted butter

3 tablespoons self-rising flour

1 tablespoon dark brown sugar

1 tablespoon cocoa powder

1 egg

1½ oz (40 g) bag chocolate-coated honeycomb candies

Chocolate Marble Cake

SERVES 1 • **PREPARATION TIME** 3 MINUTES • **COOKING TIME** 1¾ MINUTES

Beat together the butter and sugar in a 12 fl oz (350 ml) microwave-safe mug. Add the egg, vanilla extract, and flour and beat until smooth.

Microwave on full power for about 45 seconds until the mixture is just beginning to set. Scatter half the chocolate chips over the sponge and stir once or twice. Scatter over the remaining chocolate chips and stir again. Microwave for 1 minute more or until just firm to touch. Serve dusted with a little sifted confectioners' sugar.

3 tablespoons (40 g) unsalted butter, very soft

3 tablespoons superfine sugar

1 egg

¼ teaspoon vanilla extract

3 tablespoons self-rising flour

2 tablespoons bittersweet or milk chocolate chips

Sifted confectioners' sugar, for dusting

Coconut and Lime Cake

SERVES 1 • **PREPARATION TIME** 4 MINUTES • **COOKING TIME** 2 MINUTES

Put the coconut oil in a 12 fl oz (350 ml) microwave-safe mug and microwave for 20–30 seconds until melted.

Stir in the creamed coconut. Then stir in the lime zest, lime juice, and confectioners' sugar, followed by the egg white and flour. Beat together until well mixed.

Microwave on full power for 1½ minutes or until just firm to touch and a toothpick inserted into the center comes out clean.

Make the frosting. Beat together the cream cheese, confectioners' sugar, and lime juice in a small bowl until smooth. Spoon onto the cake and serve.

1 tablespoon coconut oil

1 teaspoon creamed coconut

Finely grated zest of 1 lime

2 teaspoons lime juice

3 tablespoons confectioners' sugar

1 egg white

3 tablespoons self-rising flour

For the frosting:

2 tablespoons cream cheese

1 teaspoon confectioners' sugar

½ teaspoon lime juice

19

Apple Butterscotch Cake

SERVES 1 • **PREPARATION TIME** 3 MINUTES • **COOKING TIME** 3 MINUTES

Put the apple in a 7 fl oz (200 ml) microwave-safe mug and sprinkle over the butter and sugar. Microwave on full power for 2 minutes or until the apple juices are bubbling and syrupy.

Add the flour, lemon zest, and golden raisins, then add the egg. Beat together until well mixed.

Microwave on full power for 1 minute or until risen and just firm to touch. A toothpick inserted into the center should come out clean. Serve dusted with a little sifted confectioners' sugar.

½ red dessert apple, cored and thinly sliced

2 tablespoons (25 g) slightly salted butter, cubed

2 tablespoons light brown sugar

2 tablespoons self-rising flour

Finely grated zest of ½ lemon

1 tablespoon golden raisins

1 egg

Sifted confectioners' sugar, for dusting

Peanut Butter and Jelly Muffin

SERVES 1 • **PREPARATION TIME** 4 MINUTES • **COOKING TIME** 1½ MINUTES

Put the butter and peanut butter in a 7 fl oz (200 ml) microwave-safe mug and microwave on full power for 30 seconds. Stir well.

Add the sugar, flour, and baking powder and mix until smooth. Beat in the egg.

Microwave on full power for 1 minute or until just firm to touch and a toothpick inserted into the center comes out clean.

Loosen the edges of the cake with a sharp knife and turn out onto a plate. Cut the cake in half horizontally and sandwich the layers together with the jelly. Sprinkle with a little extra sugar and serve.

1 tablespoon slightly salted butter

3 tablespoons crunchy peanut butter

1 tablespoon light brown sugar, plus extra to sprinkle

2 tablespoons self-rising flour

generous pinch of baking powder

1 egg

2 teaspoons red currant jelly

Upside-down Mango and Coconut Cake

Line the base of a 12 fl oz (350 ml) microwave-safe mug with a circle of parchment paper.

Peel the mango. Cut half the flesh into thin slices and arrange them in the base of the mug. Chop the remaining mango into small pieces and set aside.

Beat the coconut oil, confectioners' sugar, egg, flour, and coconut together in a small bowl. Stir in the chopped mango. Spoon the mixed ingredients into the prepared mug.

Microwave on full power for 2 minutes or until just firm to touch and a toothpick inserted into the center comes out clean.

Loosen the edges of the cake with a sharp knife and turn out onto a plate. Squeeze over the lemon or lime juice and sprinkle with a little sifted confectioners' sugar. Serve decorated with a sprig of mint.

½ small mango

1 tablespoon coconut oil, softened

2 tablespoons confectioners' sugar, plus extra to sprinkle

1 egg

2 tablespoons self-rising flour

1 tablespoon shredded, dried coconut

½ teaspoon lemon or lime juice

Mint sprig, to decorate

Strawberry Pimm's Cake

SERVES 1 • **PREPARATION TIME** 6 MINUTES • **COOKING TIME** 3 MINUTES

Tear the mint leaves and put them in a 12 fl oz (350 ml) microwave-safe mug. Add the sugar and use the back of a teaspoon to press the sugar into the mint to bruise the leaves. Add the dried strawberries and Pimm's.

Microwave on full power for 30 seconds. Add the butter and beat until softened, then beat in the egg and flour. Microwave on full power for 2½ minutes or until the surface feels just firm to touch and a toothpick inserted into the center comes out clean.

To serve, spoon the cream on top of the cake and sprinkle with the fruits and cucumber. Drizzle with the Pimm's and top with a sprig of mint.

3 mint leaves

2 tablespoons superfine sugar

2 tablespoons chopped dried strawberries

1 tablespoon Pimm's No. 1

3 tablespoons (40 g) unsalted butter

1 egg

3 tablespoons self-rising flour

To serve:

2 tablespoons heavy cream

2 fresh strawberries, halved

2 orange segments, chopped

1 inch (2.5 cm) piece cucumber, diced

1 teaspoon Pimm's No. 1

Mint sprig

Winter Warmer Cake

Put the coffee and measured boiling water in a 12 fl oz (350 ml) microwave-safe mug and mix together. Add the butter, sugar, cinnamon, chili powder, egg, flour, and nuts and beat together until well mixed.

Microwave on full power for 1½ minutes or until the surface feels just firm to touch and a toothpick inserted into the center comes out clean.

Spoon the cream on top of the cake and dust with a little sifted cocoa powder or drinking chocolate.

½ teaspoon instant espresso coffee granules or powder

½ teaspoon boiling water

3 tablespoons (40 g) slightly salted butter, very soft

2½ tablespoons superfine sugar

⅛ teaspoon ground cinnamon

Generous pinch of chili powder

1 egg

3 tablespoons self-rising flour

1 tablespoon chopped pecan nuts

3 tablespoons heavy cream

Sifted cocoa powder or drinking chocolate, for dusting

Pumpkin and Ginger Cake

SERVES 1 • **PREPARATION TIME** 4 MINUTES • **COOKING TIME** 2½ MINUTES

Put the butter and sugar in a 7 fl oz (200 ml) microwave-safe mug and beat until smooth. Add the egg yolk, pumpkin puree, flour, vanilla extract, and ginger and beat together until well mixed.

Microwave on full power for 2½ minutes or until the surface feels just firm to touch and a toothpick inserted into the center comes out clean.

Beat together the confectioners' sugar and preserved ginger syrup in a small bowl. Drizzle over the cake and sprinkle with extra chopped ginger, if liked.

2 tablespoons (25 g) slightly salted butter, very soft

2 tablespoons superfine sugar

1 egg yolk

3 tablespoons unsweetened pumpkin puree

2½ tablespoons self-rising flour

¼ teaspoon vanilla extract

1 inch (2.5 cm) piece preserved ginger in syrup, drained and finely chopped, plus extra to decorate (optional)

1 tablespoon confectioners' sugar

1 teaspoon preserved ginger syrup

Chocolate Crackle Cake

SERVES 1 • **PREPARATION TIME** 2 MINUTES • **COOKING TIME** 45 SECONDS

Break the chocolate into a 7 fl oz (200 ml) microwave-safe mug, then add the milk and syrup. Microwave on full power for 45 seconds, stirring once half way through cooking to make a smooth sauce.

Stir in the cereal and dried fruit. Decorate with sugar sprinkles.

1 oz (25 g) bittersweet or milk chocolate

1 tablespoon milk

1 teaspoon light corn syrup

¾ oz (20 g) crisped rice cereal

2 teaspoons golden raisins or raisins

Sugar sprinkles, to decorate

Spicy Banana Bread

SERVES 1 • **PREPARATION TIME** 3 MINUTES • **COOKING TIME** 2 MINUTES

Mash the banana in a 12 fl oz (350 ml) microwave-safe mug until almost completely pureed. Add the egg, mixed spice, butter, flour, half of the nuts, and sugar and beat together until well mixed.

Microwave on full power for 2 minutes or until just firm to touch and a toothpick inserted into the center comes out clean. Sprinkle with the remaining chopped nuts and serve drizzled with maple syrup.

1 small very ripe banana

1 egg

¼ teaspoon ground mixed spice

2 tablespoons (25 g) butter, very soft

3 tablespoons self-rising flour

1 tablespoon chopped walnuts or pecan nuts

2 tablespoons light brown sugar

Maple syrup, to drizzle

Molten Chocolate Mallow Cake

Put the butter, sugar, egg, flour, and cocoa powder in a 12 fl oz (350ml) microwave-safe mug and beat together until smooth.

Microwave on full power for 45 seconds. Cut four of the marshmallows into quarters. Add the quartered marshmallows and chocolate to the mug and stir gently to mix.

Position the remaining marshmallow on top of the mixture and microwave on full power for 1 minute or until the whole marshmallow has partially melted.

3 tablespoons (40 g) unsalted butter, very soft

2 teaspoons light brown sugar

1 egg

1 tablespoon self-rising flour

1 tablespoon cocoa powder

5 marshmallows

1 oz (25 g) milk chocolate, chopped

Juicy Fruity Cake

SERVES 1 • **PREPARATION TIME** 2 MINUTES • **COOKING TIME** 2½ MINUTES

Put the fruit smoothie and butter in a 7 fl oz (200 ml) microwave-safe mug and microwave on full power for 30 seconds.

Stir in the sugar, egg, and flour and beat together until smooth. Microwave on full power for 2 minutes. Serve dusted with a little sifted confectioners' sugar.

4 tablespoons orange and mango fruit smoothie or other fruit smoothie

1 tablespoon slightly salted butter, very soft

1 tablespoon superfine sugar

1 egg

1 tablespoon self-rising flour

Sifted confectioners' sugar, for dusting

Ricotta and Pine Nut Cake

SERVES 1 • **PREPARATION TIME** 2 MINUTES • **COOKING TIME** 1½ MINUTES

Put the ricotta, lemon zest, pine nuts, honey, sugar, cinnamon, and flour in a 7 fl oz (200 ml) microwave-safe mug and beat together. Add the egg and beat together until well mixed.

Microwave on full power for 1½ minutes or until a toothpick inserted into the center comes out clean. Decorate with the extra pine nuts and serve drizzled with extra honey.

⅓ cup (75 g) ricotta cheese

Finely grated zest of ¼ lemon

2 tablespoons toasted pine nuts, plus extra to decorate

1 tablespoon honey, plus extra to drizzle

2 teaspoons superfine sugar

Generous pinch of ground cinnamon

1 teaspoon self-rising flour

1 egg

Vegan Chai Tea Cake

SERVES 1 • **PREPARATION TIME** 3 MINUTES • **COOKING TIME** 2 MINUTES

Put the teabag and measured boiling water in a 7 fl oz (200 ml) microwave-safe mug and stir for 15 seconds. Squeeze the teabag and discard.

Add the dried fruits and mixed spice to the mug and microwave on full power for 30 seconds. Add the oil, flour, and sugar and stir until mixed.

Microwave on full power for 1½ minutes or until firm to touch and a toothpick inserted into the center comes out clean. Sprinkle with a little extra sugar and serve.

1 chai teabag

5 tablespoons boiling water

4 tablespoons mixed dried fruit

2 dried figs, sliced

¼ teaspoon ground mixed spice

4 teaspoons vegetable or canola oil

3 tablespoons self-rising whole-wheat flour

1 tablespoon turbinado sugar, plus extra to sprinkle

Vegan Apricot and Almond Cake

SERVES 1 • **PREPARATION TIME** 3 MINUTES • **COOKING TIME** 1½ MINUTES

Mix together the flour, ground almonds, and sugar in a 7 fl oz (200 ml) microwave-safe mug. Stir in the oil, soy or almond milk, and almond extract and stir well to mix. Add the apricots to the mug and stir again.

Microwave on full power for 1½ minutes or until just firm to touch. Sprinkle with the slivered almonds and serve.

2 tablespoons self-rising flour

2 tablespoons ground almonds

4 teaspoons superfine sugar

1 tablespoon vegetable or canola oil

3 tablespoons soy or almond milk

Few drops of almond extract

2 fresh apricots or 5 plump dried apricots, sliced

1 teaspoon toasted slivered almonds

Red Velvet Cake

SERVES 1 • **PREPARATION TIME** 3 MINUTES • **COOKING TIME** 2 MINUTES

Put the beet juice, butter, cinnamon, and sugar in a 7 fl oz (200 ml) microwave-safe mug. Microwave on full power for 30 seconds, then stir.

Add the nuts, egg yolk, and flour and beat together until well mixed. Microwave on full power for 1½ minutes or until just firm to touch and a toothpick inserted into the center comes out clean. Serve drizzled with maple syrup.

2 tablespoons fresh beet juice

2 tablespoons (25 g) slightly salted butter

¼ teaspoon ground cinnamon

2 tablespoons dark brown sugar

2 tablespoons chopped mixed nuts

1 egg yolk

2 tablespoons self-rising flour

Maple syrup, to drizzle

Gluten-free Black Currant Polenta Cake

SERVES 1 • **PREPARATION TIME** 3 MINUTES • **COOKING TIME** 2 MINUTES

Beat together the polenta, butter, honey, and ground almonds in a 7 fl oz (200 ml) microwave-safe mug. Add the egg and beat together until well mixed.

Microwave on full power for 1 minute. Spoon the black currants and black currant preserve on top and stir in lightly so the polenta mixture is marbled with the fruit. Microwave on full power for 1 minute. Serve drizzled with extra honey.

2 tablespoons polenta

2 tablespoons (25 g) slightly salted butter, very soft

2 tablespoons honey, plus extra to drizzle

2 tablespoons ground almonds

1 egg

2 tablespoons black currants

1 tablespoon black currant preserve

Low-sugar Spiced Passion Cake

SERVES 1 • **PREPARATION TIME** 5 MINUTES • **COOKING TIME** 2 MINUTES

Put the honey, butter, egg, flour, and ginger in a 12 fl oz (350 ml) microwave-safe mug and beat together until well mixed. Add the carrot and pineapple and mix well.

Microwave on full power for 2 minutes or until just firm to touch and a toothpick inserted into the center comes out clean. Serve topped with the cream cheese and drizzled with ginger syrup.

2 tablespoons honey

2 tablespoons (25 g) slightly salted butter, very soft

1 egg

3 tablespoons self-rising flour

1 inch (2.5 cm) piece preserved ginger in syrup, drained and chopped

2 inch (5 cm) piece carrot, finely grated

½ fresh or canned pineapple ring, chopped

1 tablespoon cream cheese

1 tablespoon preserved ginger syrup, to drizzle

No Added Sugar Date, Cardamom, and Banana Cake

SERVES 1 • **PREPARATION TIME** 5 MINUTES • **COOKING TIME** 2½–3 MINUTES

Put the dates, cardamom, and apple juice in a 12 fl oz (350 ml) microwave-safe mug.

Microwave on full power for 1 minute. Add the butter and stir until melted. Add the banana and mash well, then beat in the egg and flour.

Microwave on full power for 1½–2 minutes until just firm to touch and a toothpick inserted into the center comes out clean. Serve with Greek yogurt.

5 dates, pitted and sliced

Crushed seeds of 2 cardamom pods

3 tablespoons apple juice

2 tablespoons (25 g) slightly salted butter, cubed

½ very ripe banana

1 egg

3 tablespoons whole-wheat self-rising flour

Greek yogurt, to serve

Hot Cranberry and Apple Trifle

SERVES 1 • **PREPARATION TIME** 5 MINUTES • **COOKING TIME** 2¾–3 MINUTES

Put the apple, cranberries, lemon juice, and sugar in a 7 fl oz (200 ml) microwave-safe mug, preferably glass. Microwave on full power for 2 minutes until the fruits are soft and the syrup is bubbling. Spoon over the liqueur, if using.

Add the almonds and crumble in the cookies, then spoon the creme anglaise over the top. Microwave on medium power for 45–60 seconds until the creme anglaise is hot. Sprinkle over the extra almonds to decorate.

½ red dessert apple, cored and diced

3 tablespoons fresh or frozen cranberries

Squeeze of lemon juice

1 tablespoon superfine sugar

1 teaspoon orange or almond liqueur (optional)

1 teaspoon toasted slivered almonds, plus extra to decorate

4 amaretti cookies

3½ fl oz (100 ml) ready-made fresh creme anglaise

Cherry Chocolate Brownie Pudding

SERVES 1 • **PREPARATION TIME** 4 MINUTES • **COOKING TIME** 2 MINUTES

Break the chocolate into a 7 fl oz (200 ml) microwave-safe mug. Add the butter and microwave on full power for 45 seconds, stirring once half way through cooking to make a smooth sauce.

Stir in the cocoa powder and sugar, followed by the egg, and beat together until well mixed. Stir in the cherries.

Microwave on full power for 1¼ minutes or until risen and lightly set. Top with a scoop of ice cream and serve decorated with a fresh cherry (or two).

1 oz (25 g) bittersweet chocolate

2 tablespoons (25 g) slightly salted butter

1 teaspoon cocoa powder

2 tablespoons light brown sugar

1 egg

6 fresh cherries, pitted and halved, plus extra to decorate

Scoop of vanilla ice cream

Softly Set Raspberry Cheesecake

SERVES 1 • **PREPARATION TIME** 3 MINUTES • **COOKING TIME** 1¾ MINUTES

Put the cream cheese, sugar, egg yolk, and cream in a 7 fl oz (200 ml) microwave-safe mug and beat together until well mixed.

Microwave on full power for 45 seconds. Stir in the raspberries and microwave on full power for 1 minute or until the edges of the cheesecake are set but the center is still wobbly.

Crush the cracker or cookie, either loosely with your fingers or finely in a plastic bag using a rolling pin. Sprinkle the crumbs over the cheesecake and decorate with a few raspberries. Serve dusted with a little sifted confectioners' sugar.

Generous ¼ cup (75 g) full-fat cream cheese, softened

2 teaspoons vanilla sugar

1 egg yolk

2 tablespoons heavy cream

8 fresh raspberries, plus extra to decorate

1 graham cracker or amaretti cookie

Sifted confectioners' sugar, for dusting

Sticky Syrup Pudding

SERVES 1 • **PREPARATION TIME** 1½ MINUTES • **COOKING TIME** 1 MINUTES

Mix together the suet, flour, sugar, and raisins in a 12 fl oz (350 ml) microwave-safe bowl. Add the egg and beat together until evenly mixed.

Microwave on full power for 1 minute or until just firm to touch and a toothpick inserted into the center comes out clean.

Loosen the edges of the pudding with a sharp knife and turn out onto a plate. Spoon the syrup on top of the pudding and serve with cream or creme anglaise.

2 tablespoons shredded vegetable suet

2 tablespoons self-rising flour

1 tablespoon light brown sugar

2 tablespoons raisins

1 egg

1–2 tablespoons light corn syrup

Light cream or creme anglaise, to serve

Hot White Chocolate and Rose Mousse

SERVES 1 • **PREPARATION TIME** 4 MINUTES • **COOKING TIME** 2½–3 MINUTES

Break the chocolate into a 7 fl oz (200 ml) microwave-safe mug. Add 2 tablespoons of the cream and microwave on medium power for 1 minute, stirring half way through cooking to soften the chocolate. Stir until the chocolate has completely melted.

Add the egg yolk, rose extract, and flour and beat until well mixed.

Whisk the egg white in a small bowl until foamy and white but not peaking. Stir the whisked egg white into the chocolate mixture, lifting the sauce from the bottom of the mug into the white to combine.

Microwave on medium power for 1½–2 minutes until slightly risen and softly set. Spoon the remaining cream on top and sprinkle with rose petals.

1½ oz (40 g) white chocolate

3 tablespoons heavy cream

1 egg, separated

3 drops of rose extract

1 teaspoon all-purpose flour

Rose petals, to decorate

Vanilla Shortbread Creme Anglaise

SERVES 1 • **PREPARATION TIME** 5 MINUTES • **COOKING TIME** 4 MINUTES

Put the butter, flour, and 1 tablespoon sugar in a 7 fl oz (200 ml) microwave-safe mug and mix together. Microwave on full power for 1 minute. Spread the preserve over the top.

Beat the egg yolk, cream, milk, vanilla extract, and remaining sugar together in a small bowl. Spoon into the mug and microwave on defrost setting for 3 minutes or until the creme anglaise is lightly set. Serve dusted with a little sifted confectioners' sugar.

1½ tablespoons (20 g) slightly salted butter, very soft

3 tablespoons self-rising flour

1 tablespoon, plus 1½ teaspoons superfine sugar

1 teaspoon apricot preserve

1 egg yolk

4 tablespoons heavy cream

3 tablespoons milk

¼ teaspoon vanilla extract

Sifted confectioners' sugar, for dusting

Pear and Gingerbread Pudding

SERVES 1 • **PREPARATION TIME** 3 MINUTES • **COOKING TIME** 2¾ MINUTES

Core the pear. Cut 2 thin wedges of pear and set aside. Dice the remaining pear flesh.

Put the diced pear in a 12 fl oz (350 ml) microwave-safe mug. Sprinkle over the butter, then add the syrup, molasses, and spices. Microwave on full power for 1 minute.

Add the flour and egg and beat until well mixed. Microwave on full power for 45 seconds. Place the reserved pear wedges on top of the sponge and microwave for 1 minute. Serve drizzled with extra molasses, if liked.

½ small ripe pear

2 tablespoons (25 g) slightly salted butter, cubed

1 tablespoon light corn syrup

1 tablespoon molasses, plus extra to drizzle (optional)

¼ teaspoon ground ginger

Generous pinch of ground mixed spice

3 tablespoons self-rising flour

1 egg

Salted Fudge and Golden Raisin Pudding

SERVES 1 • **PREPARATION TIME** 3 MINUTES • **COOKING TIME** 2–2½ MINUTES

Put the butter, sugar, egg, flour, and golden raisins in a 12 fl oz (350 ml) microwave-safe mug and beat together until well mixed. Microwave for 1 minute.

Add the fudge to the mug and very gently fold into the mixture.

Microwave on full power for 1–1½ minutes until the surface feels just firm to touch and a toothpick inserted into the center comes out clean. Serve with cream.

3 tablespoons (40 g) slightly salted butter, very soft

1 tablespoon light brown sugar

1 egg

3 tablespoons self-rising flour

1 tablespoon golden raisins

1 oz (25 g) salted fudge, sliced

Light cream, to serve

Five-minute Arctic Pudding

SERVES 1 • **PREPARATION TIME** 2¾ MINUTES • **COOKING TIME** 1¼ MINUTES

Beat together the butter and sugar in a 7 fl oz (200 ml) microwave-safe mug. Add the egg yolk, flour, and vanilla extract and beat together until smooth.

Microwave on full power for 45 seconds. Push a scoop of ice cream down into the center of the mug so that it's covered with sponge mixture. (If the sponge doesn't cover the ice cream, use a teaspoon to spread some of the soft sponge over the top).

Microwave on full power for 30 seconds or until the sponge is just firm to touch. Serve drizzled with the preserve.

3 tablespoons (40 g) slightly salted butter, very soft

4 teaspoons superfine sugar

1 egg yolk

3 tablespoons self-rising flour

¼ teaspoon vanilla extract

1 scoop vanilla ice cream

1 tablespoon strawberry preserve, to drizzle

Cherry and White Chocolate Clafoutis

SERVES 1 • **PREPARATION TIME** 4 MINUTES • **COOKING TIME** 3½ MINUTES

Break the chocolate into a 7 fl oz (200 ml) microwave-safe mug. Add the butter and microwave on medium power for 1 minute, stirring once half way through cooking to make a smooth sauce.

Add the flour and stir until well mixed, then stir in the cream, egg yolk, and vanilla extract. Finally, stir in half the cherries. Microwave on medium power for 2 minutes or until very lightly set.

Sprinkle the remaining cherries on top of the clafoutis and microwave on medium power for 30 seconds. Serve dusted with a little sifted confectioners' sugar.

1½oz (40 g) white chocolate

1 tablespoon (15 g) slightly salted butter

1 teaspoon all-purpose flour

3½ fl oz (100 ml) light cream

1 egg yolk

¼ teaspoon vanilla extract

10 canned pitted cherries, drained

Sifted confectioners' sugar, for dusting

Index

Glossary

all-purpose flour : plain flour	heavy cream : double cream	self-rising flour : self-raising flour
beet : beetroot	light brown sugar : light muscovado sugar	shredded, dried coconut : desiccated coconut
bittersweet chocolate : plain chocolate	light corn syrup : golden syrup	slivered almonds : flaked almonds
black currant : blackcurrant	light cream : single cream	superfine sugar : caster suger
confectioners' sugar : icing sugar	molasses : treacle	turbinado sugar : demerara sugar
creme anglaise : custard	preserve : jam	whole-wheat flour : wholemeal flour
dark brown sugar : dark muscovado sugar	preserved ginger : stem ginger	zest : rind
golden raisins : sultanas	rolled oats : porridge oats	

Acknowledgments

Consultant Publisher: Sarah Ford
Editor: Pollyanna Poulter
Designers: Jaz Bahra and Eoghan O'Brien
Photographer: Lis Parsons
Food Stylist: Joanna Farrow
Production Controller: Sarah Connelly